101 ways to rock

ONLINE DATING

How to find love
(or not) in the digital world!

charyn pfeuffer with
dayna steele & jenny block

Daily Success
THE BOOK SERIES

101 WAYS TO ROCK ONLINE DATING
Copyright 2019 Daily Success LLC

Back cover author photo credit:
Charyn Pfeuffer - Alex Garland
Dayna Steele – Todd Parker
Jenny Block – Steph Grant

ISBN print 978-1-7337924-3-1
ISBN ePUB 978-1-7337924-4-8
ISBN MOBI 978-1-7337924-5-5

The tips in this book are merely suggestions. Because of the dynamic nature of the Internet, any Web addresses or links contained in this book may have changed since publication and may no longer be valid. The views expressed in this work are solely those of the author and do not necessarily reflect the views of the publisher, and the publisher hereby disclaims any responsibility for them.

PRINTED IN THE UNITED STATES OF AMERICA
PUBLISH DATE JULY 2019

Publisher contact and book orders:
Daily Success Publishing
957 NASA Parkway
Suite 101
Houston TX 77058
info@101waystorock.com
www.101waystorock.com

To all the beautiful humans who've taken a chance on love and algorithms – especially Alex and Jessica.

- Charyn Pfeuffer

To Wonder Husband, I said it first!

- Dayna Steele

For Robin.
Your never-ending support inspires me.

- Jenny Block

Online dating (or Internet dating) is a system that enables people to find and introduce themselves to new personal connections over the Internet, usually with the goal of developing personal, romantic, or sexual relationships.

In its purest form, dating is auditioning for mating (and auditioning means we may or may not get the part).

- Joy Browne

GETTING STARTED

By Charyn Pfeuffer

More and more people are looking for love online these days. In fact, online dating accounts for more than 25 percent of all new relationships, according to the Online Dating Association (ODA). Still, many people are left with the question, "Why can't I find a date?

Over the past two decades, online dating went from being a stigmatized way to find love to an industry that market forecasters predict will reach $3.2 billion by 2020. According to a recent Pew Research poll, 59 percent of Internet users think online dating is an excellent way to meet people.

Whether you love it or hate it, this is our new landscape for finding love. At least one-third of all marriages in the U.S. are now between partners who met online. That's more than 600,000 couples every year which would, in any other era, have remained total strangers.

Dating in today's digital world can be a demanding task. Putting your heart out there can be a scary thing – as well as wonderfully fulfilling. There isn't anything wrong with wanting to find a serious relationship from online dating. For some people, it might truly be the only way they can meet new people. *101 Ways to Rock Online Dating* will help readers demystify online dating, sort the suitors from the scammers, and learn how to connect with digital prospects in real life (IRL).

101

ways

to
rock

**ONLINE
DATING**

You have to know yourself to grow yourself.
- Dr. Juliana Morris

1

Get clear on who you are and what you really want

Online dating is a fantastic place for meeting people – if you have your priorities sorted out in advance. You need to figure out who you are and be honest with your intentions before you jump into the deep end of the dating pool. Whether you are looking for something casual, serious, or something in between, there is a site geared toward you.

Of course I am not worried about intimidating men. The type of man who will be intimidated by me is exactly the type of man I have no interest in.

\- Chimamanda Ngozi Adichie

2

Don't be intimidated

Although more people are open to searching for love online than ever before, attitudes toward online dating are still somewhat stigmatized. Some people think they are above it and can do it on their own. Others worry about what people will think. Screw it. Take a chance and see what possibilities life presents. You never know until you stretch your comfort zone. GO FOR IT. You've got this, babe.

3

Determine your deal breakers

We all have deal breakers that can ruin a relationship. It is important to figure out what those hard and fast lines are for you – whether it is having (or not having) children, political or religious beliefs, drinking and smoking habits, sexual compatibility, and more. Pinpoint what you will and will not compromise on and unapologetically stand your ground.

4

No matter your age, you are the exact right age to find love

Despite the arbitrary expiration date society places on people as they mature, you can still find and actualize a healthy, fulfilling relationship at any age. Forget every single thing culture says about being "in your prime" or gawd forbid, "past your prime." Love is boundless, and if you want to be in a relationship, you can be in a relationship – regardless of age.

5

Hire a dating coach

If you are looking for experienced, unbiased help, consider hiring a dating coach – though we think we have you covered in this book. They can help cut through the clutter and shift a client's standards, expectations, and selections based on what they actually need. By asking specific and strategic questions *before* you go on a date (most likely) based on little to no information at all, a dating coach can help cut down on time and money spent on wrong dates.

6

Use a variety of apps

Picking a dating app can be overwhelming – we get it. There are a lot of options, and the multiple signups (download the app, create a profile, add some of your favorite pictures, and write a short bio) can be tedious – not to mention the monthly fees. Define what you are looking for, then do a little research. Different apps fill different dating needs, and there are specific apps for every desire under the sun. Take your time and find the one that is right for you.

7

For mainstream dating, OkCupid is a great go-to

If OkCupid's sweet ad campaigns don't sell you, their efforts to make folks of various genders, sexual orientations, and non-monogamous life-styles feel welcome does. Whatever you're into, this site offers a lot more in-depth questioning and matching specialization than most. Again, take your time and find what works best for you.

8

Interview yourself before writing your profile

Before you sit down to write your online dating profile, brainstorm some solid interview questions. And if you are lacking insight, ask the five people who know you best to tell you what they like most about you. The best profiles can give the reader a strong sense of what a person is about, so ask yourself: What are you most proud of? What are your hobbies and interests? What are fundamental human values most important to you? What are you seeking in a partner? If you can answer and convey those ideas in a profile, you'll come across as a more well-rounded and relatable human.

9

Hire someone to write your ad

Just because you are a great person, doesn't mean you are a great writer. There is no shame in hiring someone to help you write your profile if you do not know how to describe the best version of yourself. Or you may know a writer, an author, a teacher, or someone who writes well. Ask for help! It may only cost you a bottle of wine.

10

Steer clear of overused headlines

There are zillions of daters out there in dating-land vying for your attention. "Looking for Love" or "Man Seeks Woman" is dullsville and isn't going to grab anyone's attention. A headline is a quick opportunity to make someone either roll their eyes or want to dig deeper. Take the time to write something clever and creative that will stand out. And, can we pretty please retire "Live, Laugh, Love" already? First impressions are everything.

11

Blank profiles are boring

Nothing is appealing about an empty profile. It comes across as cocky or lazy – or both. One can only imagine how much effort you will actually put into a conversation (or relationship) if you do match. *Yawn.* Instead, make your first (virtual) meet and greet as eye-catching and engaging as possible. Be confident and creative and give potential dates every reason to want to reply. It is much harder for someone to come up with a first message to you if there are only vague visual prompts about you to go on.

12

Embrace the KISS (Keep it Simple, Stupid) principle

According to a 2018 study by Microsoft, the average human being now has an attention span of eight seconds. *Gulp.* The structure of your profile is essential, so break it into 2-3 sentence mini-paragraphs at most. Most online daters tend to skim profiles for crucial information first, then go back to read the whole thing if they are interested. So, if it reads like a well-written greatest hits reel, it will be easier to digest.

Grammar is a piano I play by ear. All I know about grammar is its power.
- Joan Didion, American journalist

13

Grammar matters

As cliché as it sounds, you only get one chance to make a first impression. Your dating profile is basically a marketing package from the words you choose to the photos you pick. So, whether you like it or not, every detail is under intense scrutiny, much like a resume. Do yourself a favor and proofread your profile and look for grammar and spelling mistakes. The difference between "your" and "you're" could cost you a first date.

Personality is the glitter that sends your little gleam across the footlights and the orchestra pit into that big black space where the audience is.

\- Mae West

14

Let your personality shine

Imagine yourself sitting down to have coffee with a potential suitor. If you can write your profile almost as if you are having a conversation with the person reading it, it will make it feel as if they are really getting to know you. Write your profile as if you are writing to someone you really want to get to know.

Show the readers everything, tell them nothing.
- Ernest Hemingwaty

15

Show, don't tell

Instead of saying you are funny – or even worse, your mom, friends, or ex-girlfriend find you funny (insert eye roll here), give a punchy example that shows off your sense of humor. You will still get your point across <u>and</u> stand out from the unimaginative crowd.

If you want the right person to find you, you need to make sure you are creating a profile that is the real you. Be romantic, sassy, snarky, even cuss. Be you. Online dating gives you that opportunity. I encouraged a client to go for it when she wanted to highlight how great tits were at 47 in her profile. Her now boyfriend claims that he saw her confidence in her bold profile and contacted her immediately. You can't say the wrong thing to the right person.

- Andi Forness, online dating coach

16

Write with confidence

Whether they mean it or not, a lot of people use language that makes them seem needy or hostile. Don't use passive words, like "hope." As in, I hope to meet someone who's tall, skinny, and pretty. Instead, describe your perfect partner, "My perfect date would be…" Be assertive, confident, and say what you want, instead of getting lost in self-deprecating language. OWN YOUR WORDS.

We are constantly protecting the male ego, and it's a disservice to men. If a man has any sensitivity or intelligence, he wants to get the straight scoop from his girlfriend.
- Betty Dodson, artist, author, and sex educator

17

Represent yourself as truthfully as possible

Make sure your profile truly represents you. Use the best pictures of yourself (preferably ones that aren't 20 years old) and be super honest in your words. Let people fall for the real you.

For women, the best aphrodisiacs are words.
The G-spot is in the ears. He who looks for it
below there is wasting his time.
- Isabel Allende, author of *Of Love and Shadows*

18

Be clear about your intentions

If you are itching to get married (or remarried), say it. If you are merely looking for a good time, say it. If you eventually want kids, SAY IT. It is important to communicate where you are coming from. We don't always get what we want, and we certainly don't get it if we don't ask for it. You are worthy of all you want and need – but you have to speak up.

19

Empty adjectives don't belong in your ad

What is an "empty adjective" anyway? Basically, it is any word you use to describe yourself that can't be confirmed until someone gets to know you. Think: "I'm smart, funny, and attractive," or "I'm humble, successful, and caring." These words and phrases are all well and good, but subjective until proven otherwise.

20

You are being judged by your cover

For the love of all things date-worthy, put some creative thought into your profile photo. Nobody wants to date your dog/boat/car/group of friends, so make an effort to snap a picture of you in all your solo friendly-looking glory. A decent photo will help get your foot in the door.

21

Show your face in your photos

There are very few reasons why someone can't show their face in a dating profile. Maybe you have a high-profile job? But even then, it still feels like you're hiding something, or even worse, cheating on a significant other. If you insist on hiding your face, there better be a good explanation.

22

If you suck at taking pics, hire a photographer to take a quick series of photos

Professional photos can be a great investment. After all, a pro photographer knows how to help you pose in a way that doesn't look forced, and generally, can make you look fabulous (and perfectly lit!). The trick is to make photos look like they were taken while you were out and about, doing fun things that align with your interests and personality – and not scream "I hired a photographer for this."

Smile in the mirror. Do that every morning, and you'll start to see a big difference in your life.

- Yoko Ono

23

Smiling makes people seem more approachable

A recent experiment by Photofeeler found when you are looking at the camera, you are more attractive when you smile. There is no one-size-fits-all photo strategy, but a good rule of thumb to follow is this: If you're making eye contact, smile. If you aren't, smiling vs. not smiling doesn't matter. It's more important to determine what is appropriate and natural in context and to consider what characteristics you individually have to offer a potential partner.

24

Head-to-toe photos are effective

The online dating service Zoosk discovered using a full body shot increases messages received by 203 percent. But make sure the picture is taken in a natural setting like the beach, for example, and shows your face. A recent survey by Match.com found 29 percent of women were turned off by a photo taken in front of a mirror with a smartphone, while the 1 in 3 responding women said shirtless selfies were "downright offensive" and "an almost instant deal breaker." The takeaway? Naked, faceless torso shots are tacky.

25

Don't post group photos as your main shot

A lot of people mistakenly think including a group shot is mandatory because it makes them look more social and outgoing. Guess again. While it is true a group photo does convey those traits, it only helps you if you look great in the picture AND you're the hottest one in it. Instead, use a photo of you in a social setting, like a park or café.

26

Don't include photos with your ex cut out

If you're still friends with your ex, great. If a partner speaks about previous dates and relationships healthily and maturely, it can be a pretty good indicator of how they might treat you. Still, it is never a good idea to post a photo with an ex cropped, or even worse, blurred out.

27

Don't be a cliché

Try and avoid posting the usual visual suspects. For example, if you live in Seattle, a fish photo is almost as predictable as a shot near the Space Needle. YOU CAN DO BETTER. Use your creative capabilities.

28

Too many filters

Snapchat filters on your profile photo are a no-no. You may be hella cute IRL, but pretending to be a puppy is not.

29

Be transparent in your desires

It is okay if you to want to explore new things but be upfront about it. If you are questioning your sexuality, fine. Curious about kink? Let's talk about it. Rarely do people paint a complete picture of themselves in their online dating profile but try not to drop any major bombs.

Sexual pleasure is, I agree, a passion to which all others are subordinate but in which they all unite.
- Marquis de Sade, *The 120 Days of Sodom and Other Writings*

30

There's nothing wrong with casual sex

There is no shame in wanting straight-up sex, but a lot of people play it coy or are not willing to admit it. Instead of pretending you want some deep, heartfelt connection, what if you were honest and both daters got what they truly wanted (between the sheets)? It's a novel idea, but sometimes a physical connection does not require an emotional bond.

31

Be the single you want to meet

It's pretty commonplace to wonder if we are "worthy" or "enough," but your relationship with yourself is arguably the most critical relationship in life. The fact is, if you want a partner who understands you, you must first understand yourself. When you are the best version of yourself, the more attractive you'll become. Confidence is drop-dead sexy.

32

Let your personality show through

Playfulness is one of the most coveted charac-
ter traits for potential mates. Being silly is good
for the soul, and if you can exude whimsy in
your dating profile, that sense of feeling good
tends to beget more feeling good.

Don't get in your head about online dating and freak yourself out. Be bold and confident. Remember, everyone is as nervous as you are. Just remember, in the end, it doesn't matter. If one match doesn't work out, there will always be 10 more to take their place.

- Gigi Engle, certified sex coach, and educator

33

Don't be a negative online dater

It is such a killjoy when someone writes something like, "still not sure about online dating, but…" in their profile. *I get it.* Many people have been burned or let down while trying to date online, and sometimes, it feels more like work than play. If dating feels like a chore, don't take it out on your profile. Step away from whatever app(s) you're on and put dating on pause until you are in a more positive headspace to put yourself out there and invest in meeting people.

34

Don't say, "just ask."

If someone's on a dating app, they are most likely there to learn something about you. So please, make an effort to meet them half-way. It's mighty fine you're an "open book" and they can "ask you anything." Most people are more than willing to do the legwork once they're interested and/or invested – just give them a reason.

35

Don't tell a date what they should be like – tell them what you're like

Be confident, assertive, and make your intentions known – but don't tell potential dates who to be or what to do. The second you ask someone to swipe left or "don't message me" if they do not live up to your standards, can be a pretty major deal breaker. Instead, describe yourself in detail and let contenders decide if the dynamic is a good fit.

Money is only a tool. It will take you wherever you wish, but it will not replace you as the driver.

\- Ayn Rand

36

Don't show off material possessions

Avoid showing off material wealth in images (think expensive cars, houses, or watches), because not only does it makes you seem insecure, it tells people you have something worth trying to take.

37

Don't mention income in your profile

Avoid talking about things like financial security in your profile. It tells scammers you are worth targeting while signaling to potential dates you do not think you're good enough unless you mention you've got money. Sure, some people specifically seek a wealthy partner (and there are dating apps for that), but no matter your net worth, you are much more than your bank account balance.

38

Don't share any identifying details

You definitely want to be cautious about sharing photos that show identifying features, such as a home address, car, or license plate. Ditto for images that expose where you work or where your kids go to school.

39

Think twice before you link to Instagram

Linking your Instagram to your profile may seem like a great idea. After all, it lets you share more photos of yourself with potential matches and shows you're a real person with a real life. But be careful. Your Instagram profile probably offers a lot more information about your favorite places and activities than you realize, as well as comments made by friends and followers.

40

Recognize some people make terrible profiles, but can be fantastic dates IRL

Here's something to think about: often online chemistry has zero correlation to IRL chemistry. Sure, there are instances when you know within a few messages a match is never going to go anywhere. That's fine. But also keep in mind, sometimes, people are not the best at presenting themselves in a digital forum and do much better in person. Try to keep an open mind; you never know.

Being honest may not get you a lot of friends,
but it'll always get you the right ones.

- John Lennon

41

Have a friend give your profile a look-see

An extra set of eyes, especially if they belong to a trusted someone who will dish brutal honesty, is invaluable. Find yourself a friend who won't sugarcoat the truth and give them free rein to critique your dating profile. They may say it is a masterpiece – or it's a hot mess. Just know your real friends are looking out for you.

Everyone has inside of her a piece of good news. The good news is that you don't know how great you can be, how much you can love, what you can accomplish, and what your potential is.

\- Anne Frank

42

Have a PMA (or, Positive Mental Attitude)

The minute you stop putting yourself down and start putting yourself first (aka, stop being such a people pleaser), you will see yourself as a valuable human being – and others will too. A simple shift in attitude can affect everything from being calmer and more present on first dates to looking within for validation, and not to others. Often, the vibe we put out in the world shapes our reality, so make it a positive one whenever possible.

Trust your intuition. You don't need to explain or justify your feelings to anyone, just trust your own inner guidance, it knows best.

- Anonymous

43

Trust and listen to your gut

There are so many unknowns that come into play when you are online dating. Your intuition is primarily shaped by past experiences. If you pay attention and listen to it, your existing knowledge can help process information, like whether or not you get a sense of authenticity and transparency from a match. Go with your gut, always.

44

Make the first move

It should come exactly as no surprise a recent OkCupid study found men are more likely to send the first message on the dating website than women. Here's the thing: We are living in a "Who run the world?" landscape, so if you are interested in someone – *make a move*. Screw chivalry. Women who take charge and shift this outdated dynamic have a considerable advantage.

45

Make an effort to be original

Sure, it is intimidating to send the first message to someone you find attractive. But if you're still messaging "hey" on Tinder, it is time to rethink your opening line. Nothing makes someone unmatch another faster than a mind-numbingly boring intro. A Hinge survey found the best dating app conversations tend to lean on self-deprecation, a little vulnerability, and a willingness to dig deep into your personal history and share your most cringe-worthy moments.

Assumptions prevent us from getting to know people as individuals. Finding out and honoring how your match identifies shows respect and sets the stage for a healthy relationship where you communicate rather than assuming.

- Suzannah Weiss, feminist sex
and relationships writer

46

If you're unsure of a match's preferred pronouns, ask

The concept of gender is evolving, and therefore, so are gender identities. Asking for pronouns can prevent a person from feeling disrespected, alienated, or dysphoric (or any combination of the three) and sets an example of respect. One of the most comprehensive pronoun guides available can be found here: http://askanonbinary.tumblr.com/pronouns

47

Detach from the outcome

Once you hit send on a message to someone, *let it go.* You might hear back, you might not, so detach yourself and stop obsessing over an outcome. One person's response (or lack thereof) does not determine your desirability, so avoid getting too caught up in a single opinion.

48

Please don't pine

Online dating may increase your odds of finding love over leaving it purely to fate, but still,
it is mostly a stealth effort in fine-tuning your
approach. Instead of sitting by your computer
or smartphone, not-so-patiently waiting for a
response or overthinking what the other person
is thinking – aka "pining" – resume regularly
scheduled programming, stat. No one is a mind
reader, and until someone shares how they feel,
don't create more stress for yourself with "what
if" scenarios.

49

Don't put too much stock into online chemistry

Although many people consider love at first sight to be the holy grail of romantic experiences, the practice of online dating and mating can be awkward. We all want to feel the sizzle, that magical spark, and it is perfectly OK if a match doesn't curl your toes via text communication. Sometimes it takes a few dates for an energetic connection to click. And if it doesn't? It is perfectly fine to say, "Thanks, but no thanks" and walk away.

50

Don't invest

As a rule, it is rarely a good idea to invest in someone until you get to know them. (There are always exceptions to this rule.) Why in the world would you give a significant part of yourself to someone until you can trust it's even remotely worth it? Your heart, time, and energy are valuable, so do not spend too much time imagining the first date or introducing them to friends and family, until they have proven themselves worthy.

51

(Some) married men lie on online dating sites

A recent MSNBC survey stated that 30 percent of men using an online dating service are married. (Women aren't far behind.) If you are in an ethically non-monogamous marriage, no big deal. That is not always the case. Pay attention to details and contradictions: Blurry photos, sparse personal information, and random response times. If someone's hitched, they tend to keep their info and feelings tightly compartmentalized.

52

People may omit key details

An online dating profile is by no means a tell-all *E! True Hollywood Story*. Dating profiles do not always tell the whole truth. If someone is serious about meeting someone, they generally put their best effort into their profile. So, if you come across one that provides the most generic of detail, beware. They may not be a real human being. Or the lack of basic personal information could signal sneaky behavior. If something feels off, it probably is.

I reserve the right to love many different people at once, and to change my prince often.

\- Anaïs Nin

53

Consensual non-monogamy (CNM) is not the same as cheating

Repeat after me: CNM is not the same as cheating. It also covers a wide swath of non-traditional relationship dynamics, too many to list here. If you are interested in learning more, I suggest reading *The Ethical Slut* by Dossie Easton and Janet W. Hardy. It is 100 percent possible to have multiple romantic and/or sexual partners – at the same time – with varying degrees of emotional intimacy. As long as there is transparency and clear communication, these styles of relationships can allow partners to hold space for each other while pursuing who and what they want ethically and individually.

Question… vocally. Question the things I say, question your newspapers, television report-ers, and favorite blog. Question the things you thought and the things you think now. It's the only way any of us are going to grow… …or maybe I'm wrong.

- Stoya, author of *Philosophy, Pussycats, and Porn*

54

Do your research

There is nothing wrong with Nancy Drew-ing a match. A Pew Research Center study found 29 percent of online daters search for information about their possible dates before meeting them. If you tend to err on the side of caution (yay, you!), search engines are your friend. Look at social media profiles. You can also run a national background check online using sites like Records.com, Instant Checkmate, or Been-Verified. The name of the game is to stay safe while enjoying your date.

55

Online dating can be a catfishing playground

There are a lot of folks out there who prey on lonely people. Catfishing, or the fine art of pretending to be someone you are not, to lure someone you've never met into a relationship, is a strange online phenomenon. If someone has a too-good-to-be-true sob story and makes financial requests, run far, far away – especially if they shy from meeting in person. If your internal radar sets off any red flags – *ever* – listen.

56

Another sleuthing option is a reverse image search

If you come across a photo that seems suspect, use a reverse image search engine to see if it's for real. Google Images allows people to reverse photo search by uploading an image from your computer or pasting the link of the image in the search bar itself. Or you can simply drag and drop the image in the search bar. On mobile devices, it works best by using a third-party service called Labnol (https://www.labnol.org/internet/mobile-reverse-image-search), which is a free website that uses the same Google Images reverse search engine but also works on mobile browsers.

57

When in doubt, set up a video chat

Okay, this may sound extreme. But, if you have any whiff of uncertainty about meeting someone in person, request a pre-date Skype or Face-Time call. Don't waste anyone's time and don't let them waste yours. A few minutes of virtual face time can cement whether or not you want to invest your precious time in coffee or a meal with someone.

58

Never send money to someone you've met online

AARP looked at how often U.S. adults ages 18 and over were targeted or victimized in online relationship scams. 27 percent indicate they or someone they know has encountered an online relationship scam. Fifty-seven percent of those scammed lost money or suffered other financial losses. All up, dating fraud has increased by 32 percent since 2015. Never send money to someone you have met online, no matter what reason they give or how long you've been speaking to them.

59

Fakers are no fun

Fakers are the people out there who really don't want to date. They want to text or message you all day long, but when it comes down to pulling the trigger to make an IRL date, they flake. They tend to be introverts, who really at the end of the day, really just want another a human being to connect with – virtually. They're also the person who is briefly in town for business. They may be coupled at home, but when they breeze through town, they are looking for a quick and easy local thing.

60

Don't move a conversation off an app until you're confident the person is who they say they are

A lot of people are quick to try and push a conversation off an app and into real life. Sure, it makes sense. It takes a lot of effort to manage messages, especially if you are on multiple dating apps and don't check them often. There is something intimate though about giving a match digits, so make sure your date is who they say they are before giving out any personal details.

61

Do not send dick pics

I do not care how proud you are of your penis. Most veiny one-eyed monsters are not particularly attractive in and of itself. Sending unsolicited dick pics is not only creepy, but it's also non-consensual. Also, it is the fastest way to kill a conversation. Like, would you pull your junk out in public on a first date? Because basically, it is the same, highly inappropriate behavior. Repeat after me 100 times: DON'T SEND DICK PICS.

62

Check your misogyny at the door

Misogyny reveals itself in many ways and devaluing the time of women is one (see: ghosting.) Refusing to take accountability when called out on sexist behavior is another. It does not matter what you're looking for dating-wise. There is a way to do it without making another person feel like garbage. It's called healthy communication.

63

Ditto for racism

Racism and intolerance are absolute no-gos when it comes to dating. This is not up for debate.

64

Ask questions

Get the conversation flowing by referencing your match's profile and asking questions. Keep the tone light and avoid any "job interview" style interrogations. There is a big difference between asking playful, curious questions and asking loaded questions that require someone to defend themselves. (The latter is lame and no way to start a get-to-know-you type conversation.)

Have enough courage to trust love one more time and always one more time.

\- Maya Angelou

65

Don't think dating is easy after a serious relationship.

It is easy to compare a new date to an old relationship. But, it's important to keep in mind this is a brand-new person with different values, behaviors, and personality. Treat this relationship as a bright and shiny new entity instead of focusing on former loves. When we focus on the old, we often block ourselves from fully experiencing the here-and-now and potential to find new love.

66

Don't make any assumptions

Getting to know someone is hard, and bringing pre-judgments to the table does not help. Here are a few that come to mind: You may have learned certain life lessons faster than others, but do not underestimate what the other person has experienced. Don't assume every date will be a fairytale. Let the magic happen, but do not expect it. Also, do not assume you know someone's "type." There are *so* many variables that make a person. Try to keep an open heart and mind.

67

Resist dating someone who reminds you of your ex

When we look back on our dating resume, there is usually a distinct pattern in our choice of partners. Sometimes, we get it right; sometimes, we get it wrong. If you had an amicable split with a partner whom you still think is terrific, there are no real warning signs this type is wrong for you. However, if you have had a series of bad relationships with a similar kind of person, you may want to rethink your dating strategy.

68

Be an ally

If you are dating online, chances are you will encounter people from different cultures and backgrounds. There are so few safe spaces for marginalized populations to make meaningful connections – please be kind and mindful of inclusion. Pay attention to what you say and be open to correction. Even the most well-meaning people make mistakes. Every single person deserves the opportunity to connect and find romance with someone who respects and appreciates them.

69

Don't assume single, non-monogamous women want to be your unicorn

If you are a non-monogamous couple, do not assume every single, non-monogamous woman wants to be your unicorn, aka the hard-to-find female in the world of swingers and open relationships. If you are a noncommittal woman who gets off on giving and receiving, there's nothing quite as satisfying as giving pinch-hit pleasure. But it is never, ever a given.

70

Don't yuck someone else's yum

Do not do it. Like, ever. Just because you don't like something doesn't mean everyone else should dislike it. (Unless it's blue cheese, then, despite unpopular opinion, it's perfectly OK.) There is a big wide world out there of interests, and judging other people's sexuality, gender expression, or relationship agreements does not provide a safe space to develop feelings. Pretty please, let's put an end to sex snobbery.

71

If you're dating pre-divorce, be sure your marital relationship is complete.

If you are trying to date while in the throes of a divorce, ask yourself: Is my marital relationship over even though my divorce isn't final? Have I kicked all the emotional debris from my nearly-dead dynamic to the curb? And, most lawyers will frown on dating before your paperwork is official. Flirtation and sexy time can make you feel attractive and desirable again just make sure your timing is good.

72

Be aware of "wounded" daters

Wounded daters are often in a state of transition. They are coming off another relationship, maybe a divorce. Or they are living with a core wound that's been festering for a long time. Instead of healing and becoming a whole adult, they often keep a great emotional distance and wait-and-see to expose any real feelings to avoid hurt. Basically, this is fear-based dating at its finest.

73

"No" is a complete sentence

If you have ever felt harassed on an online dating site, you're not alone. The Pew Research Center found 28 percent of online daters have felt harassed on online dating sites (and that is only the people who reported it). Whether you have been the recipient of indecent remarks or unsolicited NSFW photos, remember this undesirable behavior is problematic. You never have to explain or justify why you want someone to stop. "No" is always a complete sentence.

74

Don't be afraid to meet up IRL early

Instead of getting caught up messaging non-stop, make a plan early on to meet in person. It is easier to get a gauge on someone once you have met face-to-face, and if you're going back-and-forth for weeks, the less likely you are to follow through. But, as we mentioned in a previous tip, just be sure the person is who they say they are.

75

Arrange for your own transportation

Once upon a time, it was commonplace to get picked up for a first date. In an era of electronic courtship, not so much. I know the "want to meet me there?" mindset is maddening for some. But from a safety perspective, it makes a lot of sense – at least until you've met someone IRL. Avoid letting someone know exactly where you live until you know them better.

76

Have a go-to spot for first dates

It is super important for me to feel safe on a first date. So unless your date has their heart set on a particular activity, make a (well-vetted) suggestion. Opt for a public place, close to home, and where there will most likely be a familiar face in case things go south. Having an extra layer of personal comfort and security will significantly reduce your first date angst.

77

If you're sober or in recovery, suggest a dry date

An easy way to maintain sobriety is to avoid situations where alcohol is present. Think daytime dates that are more activity focused. If things progress, you'll need to be honest about the fact you're in recovery. Vulnerability can be scary, but how the other person responds can give great insight into your relationship potential. If someone has an issue with your sobriety, they clearly aren't the right person for you.

78

Go on as many first dates as possible

Cast a wide net and keep reaching out because online dating is a skill you develop over time. The more people you go out with, the more self-aware you will be, and the better quality dates you will have. Try not to give up after a few less-than-stellar experiences. Remember, practice makes perfect and will help you be a better version of yourself. You only need to meet one person who could change your life forever.

79

Act like it's a second date

To minimize first date awkwardness, imagine you are meeting up with a friend you've known forever. By the time you've hatched plans for a first date, there is usually some underlying sense of familiarity. Make that knowledge work for you. When you can pretend you've known someone for years, it impacts your body language and facial expressions in a positive manner.

80

Swap online dating war stories

This may be a controversial stance, but every single person who dates online has a story. I am not a fan of bringing all the baggage to the first date table, but swapping online dating war stories is an easy thing to bond over.

81

Always put yourself first

If something feels off, it is your right to leave (whether it's an online conversation or an actual date). If you encounter problematic behavior on an app, report and block the person immediately. If you are on a date IRL, it's OK to call for a ride or have a friend meet you. How you leave is up to you, and you should never apologize for putting yourself first.

82

You can change your mind

Wrapping up a date when you know you don't want a second one is always awkward. If you are not feeling it, instead of over-promising and never delivering, a simple "I'm no longer interested, but I wish you all the best" is the right thing to do. And if you lose interest before the first date rolls around, spare everyone's feelings, and cancel plans. There is no need to lie or give a reason why. No hearts will be broken.

83

Don't intentionally waste anyone's time

One of the most terrible trends in online dating is "ghosting," or ending a relationship with someone by cutting off communication without explanation. We're living in a disposable dating culture where people meet, go out, maybe make out, then never speak again. Permanence isn't exactly a strong suit for a lot of modern-day daters, but you don't have to be rude about it.

84

Beware of breadcrumbing

Breadcrumbing, defined by Urban Dictionary as "the act of sending out flirtatious, but non-committal text messages (i.e., "breadcrumbs") to lure a sexual partner without expending much effort," equates to leading someone on. Basically, breadcrumbers will send sporadic messages, slide into your direct messages (DMs) every so often, and like your social media posts when the mood strikes. If you're looking for a steady connection, there's nothing reliable about these folks who semi-try to stay relevant.

85

Leave your baggage at home

For your first few dates, keep it positive. Wait and see if you can simply have fun together before you share your bloodiest war stories. We all have baggage and insecurities from our past – from failed relationships to fears of commitment. But to succeed in the dating world, you need to be willing to leave it behind, at least until you go deep with someone new. The thing is – *everyone* has baggage. Don't let it keep you from finding future happiness.

86

Listen to your date

If your date says they want to limit how much they drink or get home a little earlier so they can wake up for work the next morning, respect and support it. Don't pressure them into staying out longer or having another drink. Listen and respect what they say.

87

Conversation may be a little awkward.

Best case scenario? Conversation flows naturally. How long have you lived here? Where was your last trip? What kind of music do you like? If communication doesn't flow and there are moments of awkward silence, that's OK. You are basically starting at square one in getting to know one another. Ask questions and listen to their answers. Curiosity can go a long way in sidelining any weirdness.

Consent can be sexy! Reframing a question as part of seduction/foreplay allows couples to be clear about what kind of sexual activity is allowed while keeping the mood alive. Saying, "I'm wondering what it would be like to kiss you" in a soft, seductive tone can feel easier (and hotter) in a steamy moment than, "Do you mind if I kiss you?"

- Elle Chase, author of *Curvy Girl Sex: 101 Body-Positive Positions to Empower Your Sex Life*

88

Always ask for consent

The Merriam-Webster Dictionary defines "consent" as "to give assent or approval." In simple terms, consent is clear, enthusiastic, and communicated. A big myth in our society is that talking about consent ahead of time ruins the vibe. There's nothing sexier than someone asking permission if it's okay to hug, kiss, or touch another person. Also, remember from an earlier tip, "no" is a complete sentence. End of story.

Your standards are yours, and they assist in letting you feel comfortable and safe – and not just from STIs.
- Carol Queen Ph.D.,
Good Vibrations Staff Sexologist &
Curator of the Antique Vibrator Museum

89

Define your safer sex standards

Before you find yourself hot, bothered, and horizontal, get clear on what your safer sex standards are. This could mean seeing STI test results from any potential new partner to using barriers for penetrative sex. STI is a sexually transmitted infection. As opposed to an STD, an STI might never produce symptoms or develop into a disease. Sure, it can be awkward to talk about safer sex protocols, but it's essential, and it gets easier with practice. If a partner does not respect your safer sex standards, they may not recognize other boundaries either. Take note.

Saying 'I'm clean' is very often misunder-stood, yet widely used. What people typically mean who say 'I'm clean' is they haven't seen any symptoms they believe are sexually transmitted diseases on their genitals.
- Nicole Prause, Ph.D., and founder of Liberos

90

Sexually transmitted disease (STD) statuses aren't "clean" or "dirty."

A big pet peeve for many is when people refer to an STD status as being "clean." If being STD-free makes you "clean," does having one make you "dirty"? In the U.S., 110 million people — about one-third of the population — have an STD at any given time. Often the social stigma surrounding STDs is more damaging than the disease itself.

91

Who pays for the first date?

A lot of people believe whoever initiates the first date should be prepared to pay for it. A Money and SurveyMonkey study illustrates a more traditionalist viewpoint: 78 percent of respondents said they think men should pay for the first date. When the bill is dropped, avoid turning the moment into a big dating test. If picking up the tab or splitting the bill is prohibitively expensive, there's nothing wrong with having a budget-friendly first date that avoids the bill situation altogether, like going for a walk. And if someone does treat you, the most gracious response is always "thank you."

92

It's OK to end a not-so-great date

We're a big fan of the one-and-done-drink-bailout. If you're totally underwhelmed by your date, 30 minutes – or the approximate time it takes to suck down one drink – is enough of an investment before deciding to cut and run. Just don't be a jerk about it.

93

Don't create a fantasy after two dates

The temptation to fantasize can intensify when you have met someone online. (You shouldn't do this offline either.) Sometimes we get so tired of dating we just want to be done with it and fast forward to the next big thing: the actual relationship. But getting too attached too soon is often the worst thing that can happen to a budding connection. Getting to know another person, truly, takes time and patience. Take a deep breath and count to 10 before you turn into a walking rom-com trope.

94

Safety first

The reality is every 98 seconds an American is sexually assaulted. One in five women will be raped within their lifetime (compared to 1 in 71 men.) Set up a virtual buddy system with a trusted friend and check in at set times. Another option is to use a location sharing app, like Find My Friends or Google Maps.

95

You can sleep with someone on the first date

Everyone has heard the rule: Don't sleep with someone until the third date. A recent survey of 1,000 18- to 35-year-old women found that over 83 percent felt men will lose interest and respect if you hook up with them too soon. But 70 percent of men said it's not true – if they're interested, it doesn't matter. Ditch the so-called rules of dating and do what feels right for you. As long as it is safe and consensual, who cares?

96

Or - don't have sex until you're ready

At some point, dating will most likely lead to sex. But remember, there's no need to rush it. Be upfront with your partner about your feelings toward sex and spell out what you are and are not comfortable with (aka, establish boundaries). This kind of constructive communication can help develop trust with a partner. And if you're not interested in sex, that's OK too. There's no one Little Black Dress approach to relationships, and you can DIY whatever dating style suits you best.

This is a good sign,
having a broken heart.
It means we have
tried for something.
- Elizabeth Gilbert

97

Rejection will happen

If you haven't experienced dating rejection in a while, it can be discouraging. The key is not to take it personally, as it more than likely has nothing to do with you. Sometimes, the person feels merely a friendship vibe. And if you are the one not interested, instead of pulling a Houdini act (which almost always results in icky feelings for someone or both), be a good human being put a clean end to any relationship, no matter how short. It's the kind thing to do.

98

Online dating fatigue is real

The whole selling point of dating apps is: "Oh, look! It's sooo quick, easy, and convenient to meet someone." And depending upon what you're looking for, sometimes it is. But a lot of the time, online dating is sifting through a whole bunch of crap to find a real possibility. Sometimes, it feels like you're one of the last people at the bar trying to take someone home before closing time – which can be exhausting. When online dating burnout hits, take a break. Then, get back out there again.

99

Be nice

Researchers at Michigan State University claim to have found the key to long-lasting devotion: find a nice person, rather than someone with similar interests or a compatible personality. The study looked at more than 2,500 couples who've been married for roughly 20 years and showed having a partner who's nice leads to higher levels of relationship satisfaction. The takeaway? It's simple. Don't be a dick.

100

But if you like someone, say so

If you like someone, say so. Life is short, and if you wait for things to happen, you may miss out. Instead, pick your moment and tell them you'd like to see them again. (Text is perfectly OK if in-person is too terrifying.) Try not to build it up too much in your head. Remember, no matter what happens, life will go on, but you won't have to live with any "what if" regret.

101

Download "Cheap Thrills" by Sia

If you are looking for inarguably the world's most perfect song to swipe to, "Cheap Thrills," the sixth track from Sia's seventh studio album, *This Is Acting*, is it. It is written in common time of 90 beats per minute, making it the perfect song for swipers who don't want to waste time. Fun fact: Brittany Spanos of *Rolling Stone* called it a "bouncy party anthem."

To find your prince,
you have to kiss
a lot of frogs.
- Anonymous

ABOUT THE AUTHORS AND 101 WAYS TO ROCK CREATORS

CHARYN PFEUFFER is a feminist writer and sex educator. She got her start in journalism 20 years ago running the Personals & Promotions department at the *Philadelphia Weekly*, where she penned the popular sex and dating advice column, "Ask Me Anything." More than 20 years later, her work has appeared in more than 100 outlets, including AARP, BravoTV, Brides, The Globe and Mail, Kinkly, Marie Claire, Playboy, Refinery29, SheKnows, Thrillist, and The Washington Post. Charyn lives in Seattle with her rescue dog, Mimi.

charynpfeuffer.contently.com/
charynpfeuffer@gmail.com
Twitter: @Charyn Pfeuffer
Instagram @supergoodsex
Facebook and LinkedIn: Charyn Pfeuffer

DAYNA STEELE, the creator of the *101 Ways to Rock* book series**,** is a Texas Radio Hall of Famer, serial entrepreneur, popular motivational speaker and author of many books on success including *Rock to the Top: What I Learned about Success from the World's Greatest Rock Stars*. Dayna also created and writes *Your Daily Success Tip*, business and life success tips enjoyed by thousands of people and companies every weekday. She lives in Houston, Palm Springs, and New York with her "Wonder Husband" and various rescue animals. Dayna ran for the US Congress in 2018 in Texas.

www.yourdailysuccesstip.com
info@daynasteele.com
Twitter: @daynasteele

Instagram: @daynasteele
Facebook and LinkedIn: Dayna Steele

JENNY BLOCK is a writer, speaker, and the lead recruiter for *101 Ways to Rock* authors. She is the author of three books, and her work appears in and on a variety of high-profile websites and publications including *Huffington Post, Yahoo Travel, The Daily Meal, Playboy, Swaay,* and *American Way.* Jenny is also often called on as an expert for *Cosmopolitan, SheKnows, Huffington Post,* and many others. She speaks on cruises, as well as at bookstores, conferences, resorts, and many other events. She lives on the water in Southeast, TX with her wife and their chi-terrier Walter.

www.thejennyblock.com
jennyeblock@mac.com
Twitter: @Jenny_Block
Instagram: @thejennyblock
Facebook and LinkedIn: Jenny Block

PUBLISHER CONTACT INFORMATION
AND LARGE QUANTITY BOOK ORDERS

Daily Success Publishing
957 NASA Parkway
Suite 101
Houston TX 77058
info@101waystorock.com
www.101waystorock.com

NOTES:

NOTES:

NOTES:

How it all began ....

The *101 Ways to Rock* book series all started with Dayna Steele's book, *101 Ways to Rock Your World: Everyday Activities for Success Every Day.* It grew from there. The possibilities of titles and tips are endless. Why? Because everyone is an expert at something. Yes, that means you. Have an idea for 101 ways to rock the world? Let us know: info@101waystorock.com.

In the meantime, here's an excerpt from that first book. You'll find the entire book available for free on Smashwords.com. Enjoy!

101 Ways to Rock Your World:
Everyday Activities for Success Every Day

Your Daily List

The Merriam-Webster dictionary defines *success* as "a favorable or desired outcome; also, the attainment of wealth, favor, or eminence."

In March 2011, I wrote a simple blog post for FastCompany.com as a part of their "Expert Leaders" (now Expert Perspective) blog series. "5 Things to Do Every Day for Success" was inspired by several conversations with friends, family members, and audience participants after my speech presentations about how to be successful. Most of those conversations started with this question: "You seem to be doing well. How do you do it?"

If you have enough of those conversations, you start to realize "success" is no different from the elusive Holy Grail: many want it but don't know where to find it or how to achieve it—or, more importantly, where to start.

The beginning of any success story is to set a strong foundation and create a "personal brand" for you. You create or start both by habit, consistency, reliability, and creativity—every day.

I wrote the FastCompany.com post as a simple list of how to get started on everyday success with these simple everyday activities:

- Wake up early.
- Review the news.
- Send something to someone who can give you money for your product or service.
- Contact an old acquaintance you have not spoken with in a while.
- Write a handwritten note to someone.

Then the strangest, most wonderful thing happened with the original blog post. It struck a chord with people around the world and started to go "viral" in May 2011, then again all summer and fall of that year, and as of this writing, it remains in the top ten most-read posts for the FastCompany.com "Expert Leaders" (now Expert Perspective) blog series. It appears people just need a starting point to reach their own success in terms they can understand and can start with immediately. It was that simple.

Success can mean many things to many people, but ultimately, success is defined as what makes you happy and satisfied with your own life. Whether you want to be Steve Jobs, Warren Buffett, or Bill Gates, or just pay your bills and have time to play, the suggestions in this book will help you set a foundation for success each and every day in whatever you do.

There will be the naysayers who say this list is too simple, that these are things you should have learned from your parents or early on in your career. (See what I have to say about this in #83.) There will be those who say there is no way you can do all 101 suggestions in this book every day. Then there will be the others who will attempt to do all 101 suggestions in this book every day until they drive themselves, and everyone around them, crazy.

What I suggest is that you read the book and start to incorporate the suggestions into your daily routine until they become habit. Once you do so, you will not need the list anymore. You will be too busy being successful to worry about anything else. Simply put, you must be brilliant at the basics in order to succeed at the next level.

Most importantly, just as beauty is in the eye of the beholder, remember that success can only be defined by you.

> *It is amazing how many people are*
>
> *too busy to succeed.*
>
> —Dave Ramsey

Five Things to Do Every Day for Success
Originally posted on FastCompany.com

1. Wake up early.*
For the next week, get up half an hour earlier than you normally do ... *and get going!* If you get a few more things done, then get up even earlier the next week. Early in the morning is a great time to get work done because most of your associates have not started emailing, tweeting, calling, texting, or posting yet.

*This, by the way, is the number one activity or tip others want to argue with me about. So, let me clarify. Be up well before the people who give you money

(customers, clients, fans) and before your competition. If your fans (again, customers and clients) work and give you money during the day, then get up early in the morning. If they give you money at night, well, lucky you, you get to sleep in.

> *The ability to convert ideas to things*
> *is the secret to outward success.*
> —Henry Ward Beecher

2. Pay attention to the news.

Read the headlines and watch the news. You will not only know what is going on in the world but will also be the first to recognize opportunities for you and your business (if you followed #1) long before the competition has even had their first cup of coffee.

3. Get in touch with someone you have not talked to in a while.

Touch base with old friends or associates you have not talked to in ages. Ask how they are, what they are working on, and ask or suggest how you might help. You will make their day. You will have also added another person to your current network of people you know. Remember the old show business saying: "It's not what you know but who you know."

> *Always bear in mind that your own*
> *resolution to succeed is more*
> *important than any one thing.*
> —Abraham Lincoln

4. Send something to someone who can give you money.

Send something to one person who can hire you or buy your product at some point in the future. Maybe it is something you promised to follow up with, a quick e-mail with a link to something relevant, or a "Hey, just checking in to see how things are going" e-mail. It could also be a birthday card, an invoice, a gift, a lead, a client, an interesting link—anything. This will keep you top-of-mind with this person, and that is a good thing when he or she gets in the mood to spend some money.

5. Write a handwritten note to someone.

Seriously. It is a lost art and makes quite an impression. There is always someone you can send a note to, whether it is a thank-you note, a birthday card, or just a "hello" note. The fact it is handwritten makes a powerful impact on the receiver, and it also stands out in the mound of junk mail we receive weekly. I promise a handwritten note will not go unnoticed.

COMING FALL 2019
101 WAYS TO ROCK SOLO
FEMALE TRAVEL
Pre-order now wherever books
are sold!

Daily Success
THE BOOK SERIES